RETRO

NOMADS

retro1

/ˈrɛtrəʊ/

Learn to pronounce

adjective

adjective: **retro**

1. 1.
   imitative of a style or fashion from the recent past.
   "retro 60s fashions"

synonyms:

in period style, period, nostalgic, evocative, of
yesteryear, olde worlde;
dated, old-fashioned, backward-looking, retrogressive,
out of date, passé
"a retro restaurant with a Fifties-style lunch counter"

noun

noun: **retro**

1. 1.
   retro clothes, music, or style.
   "a look which mixes Italian casual wear and American
   retro"

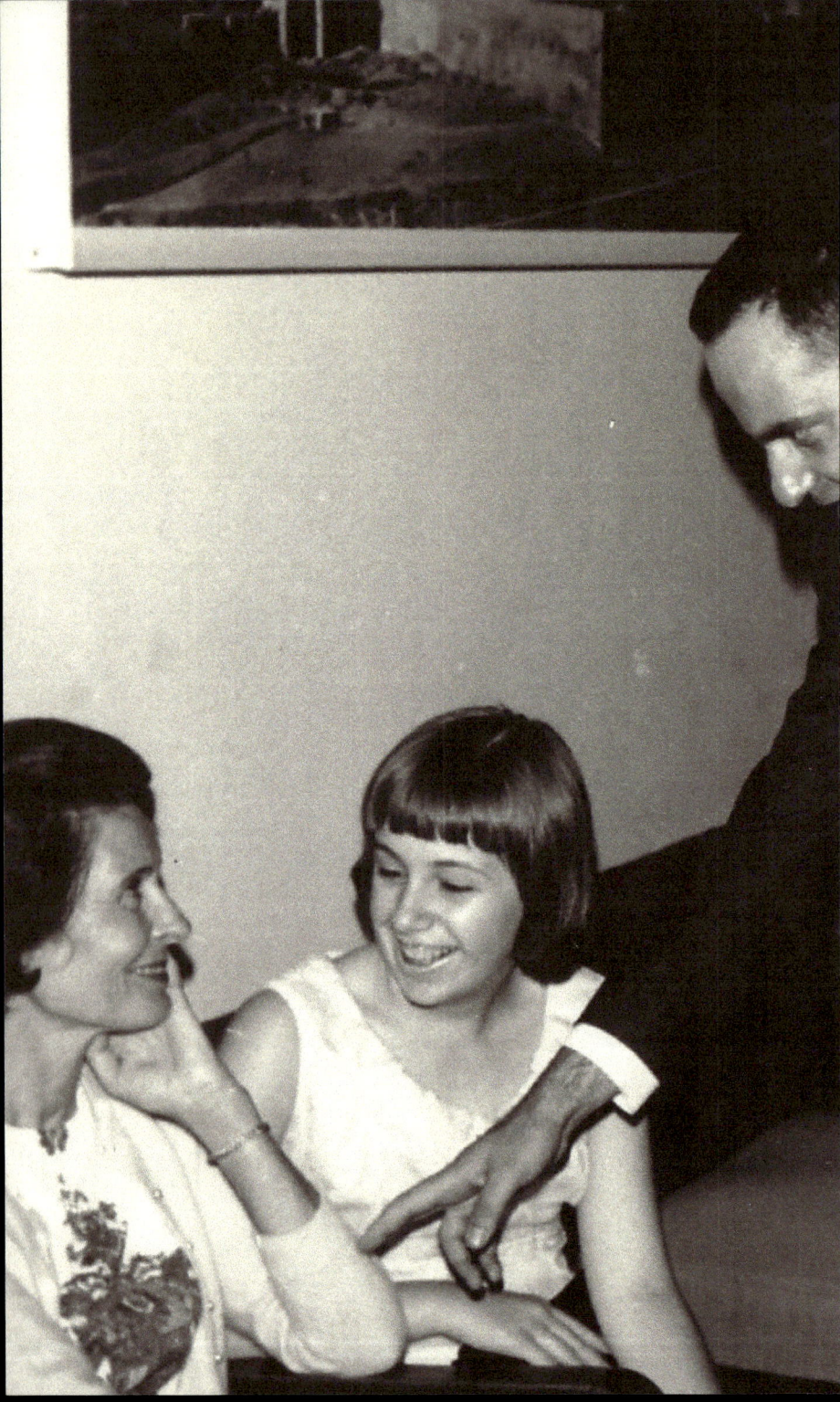

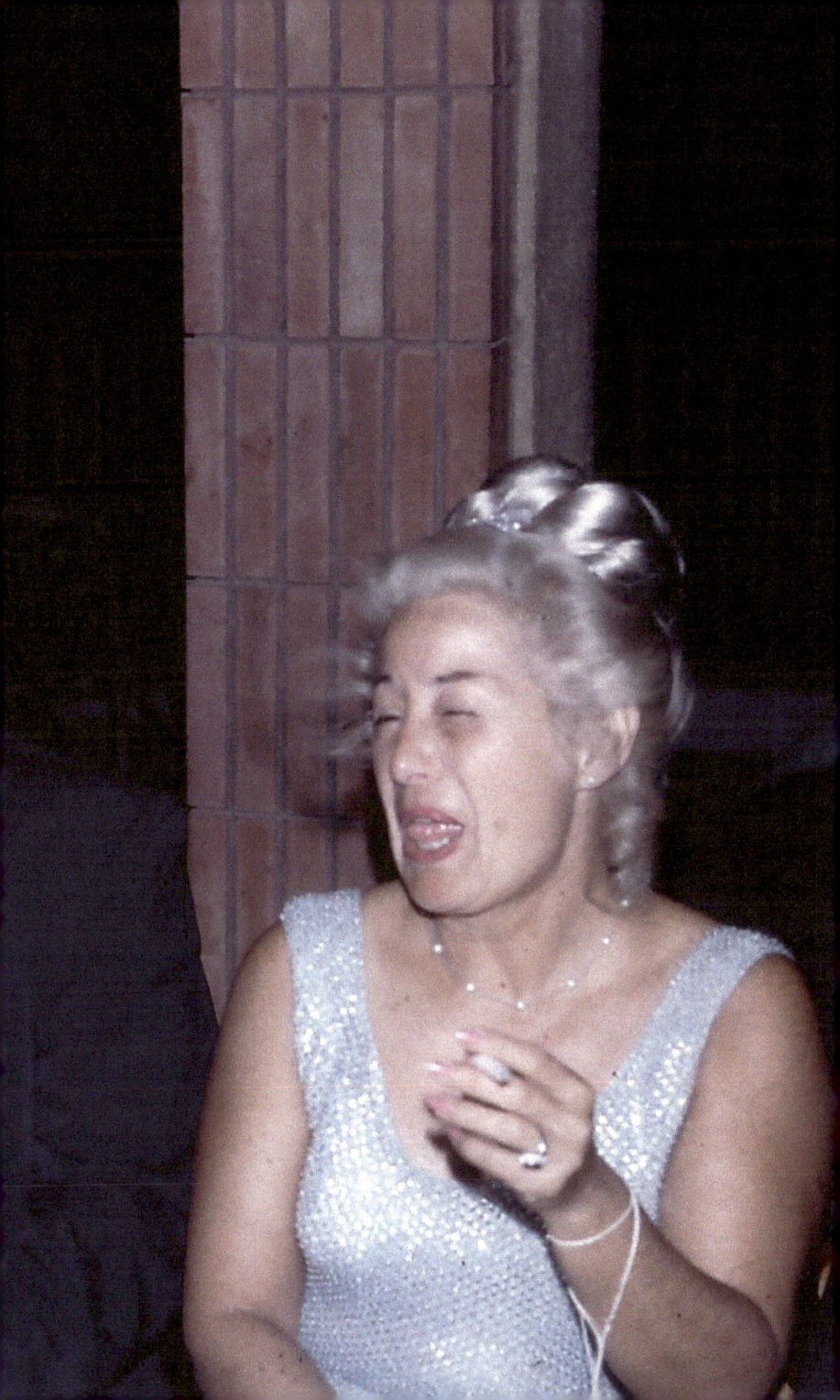

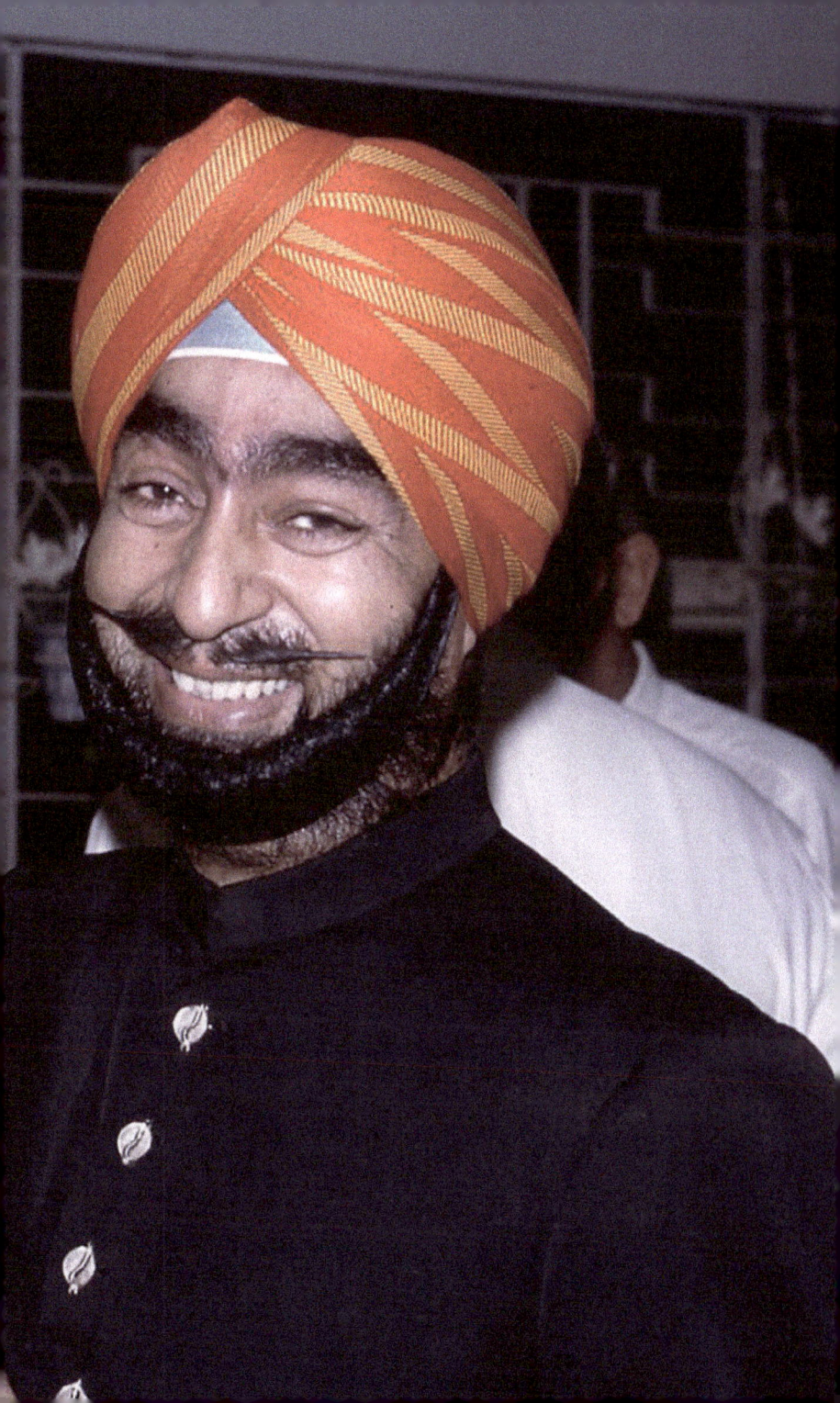

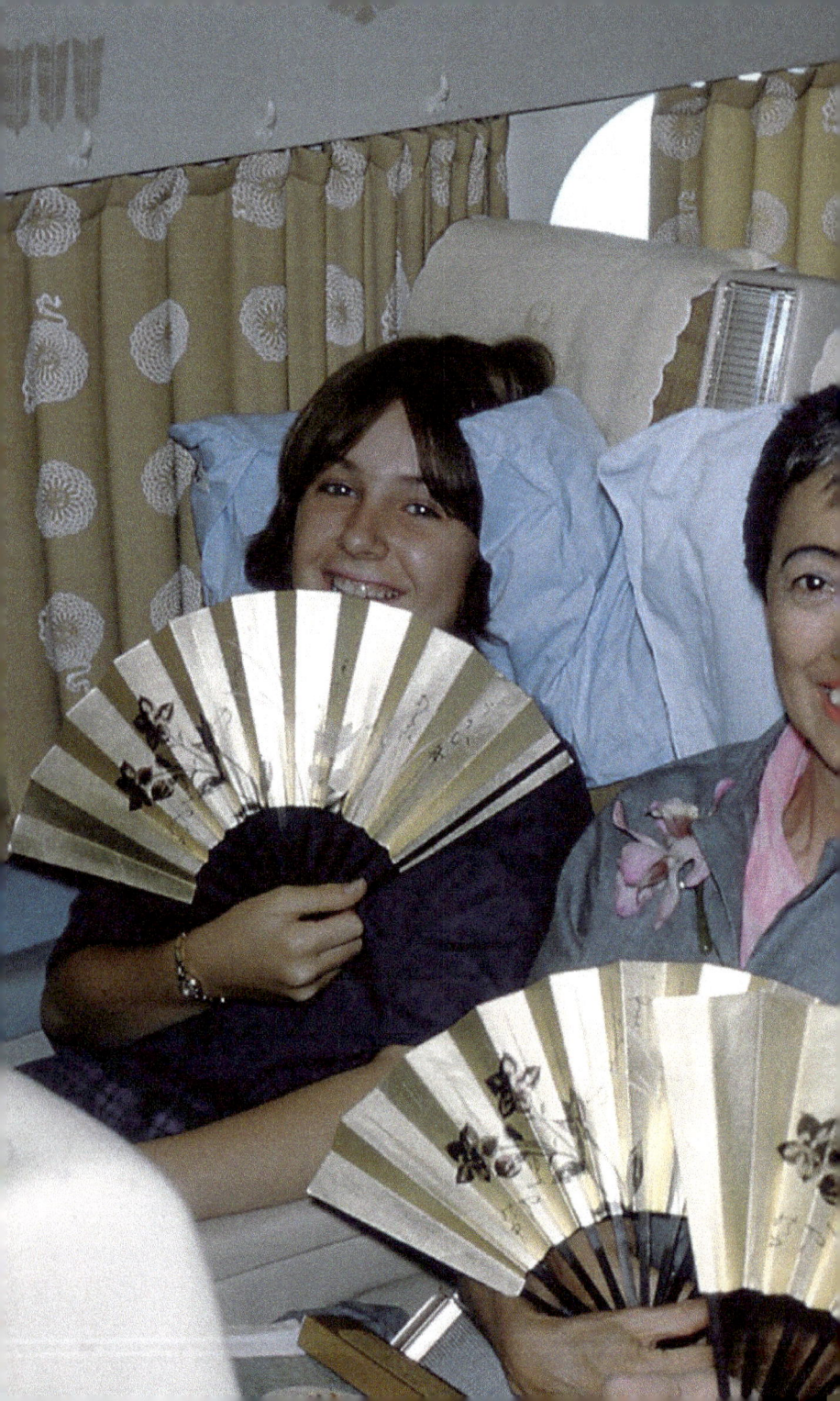

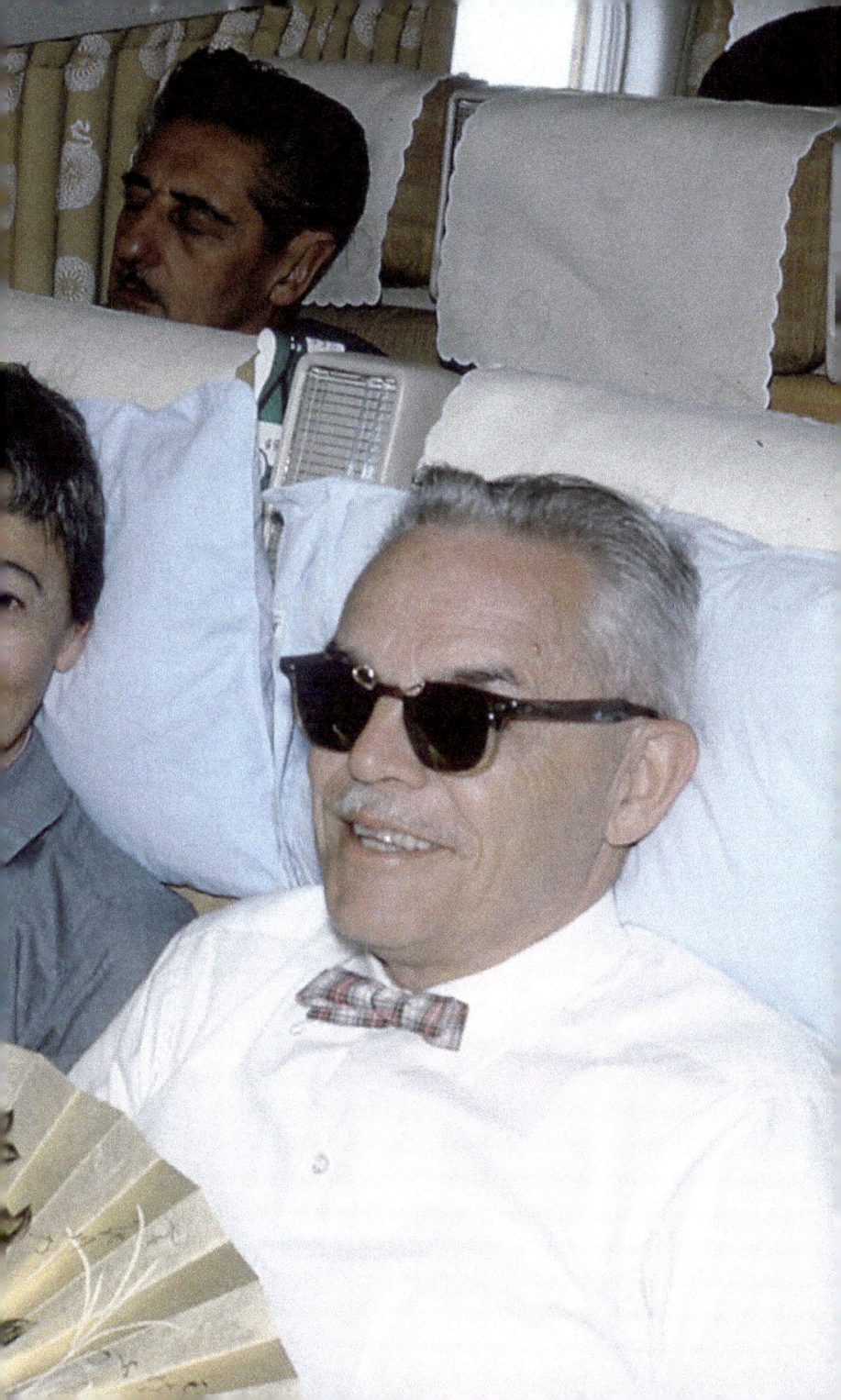

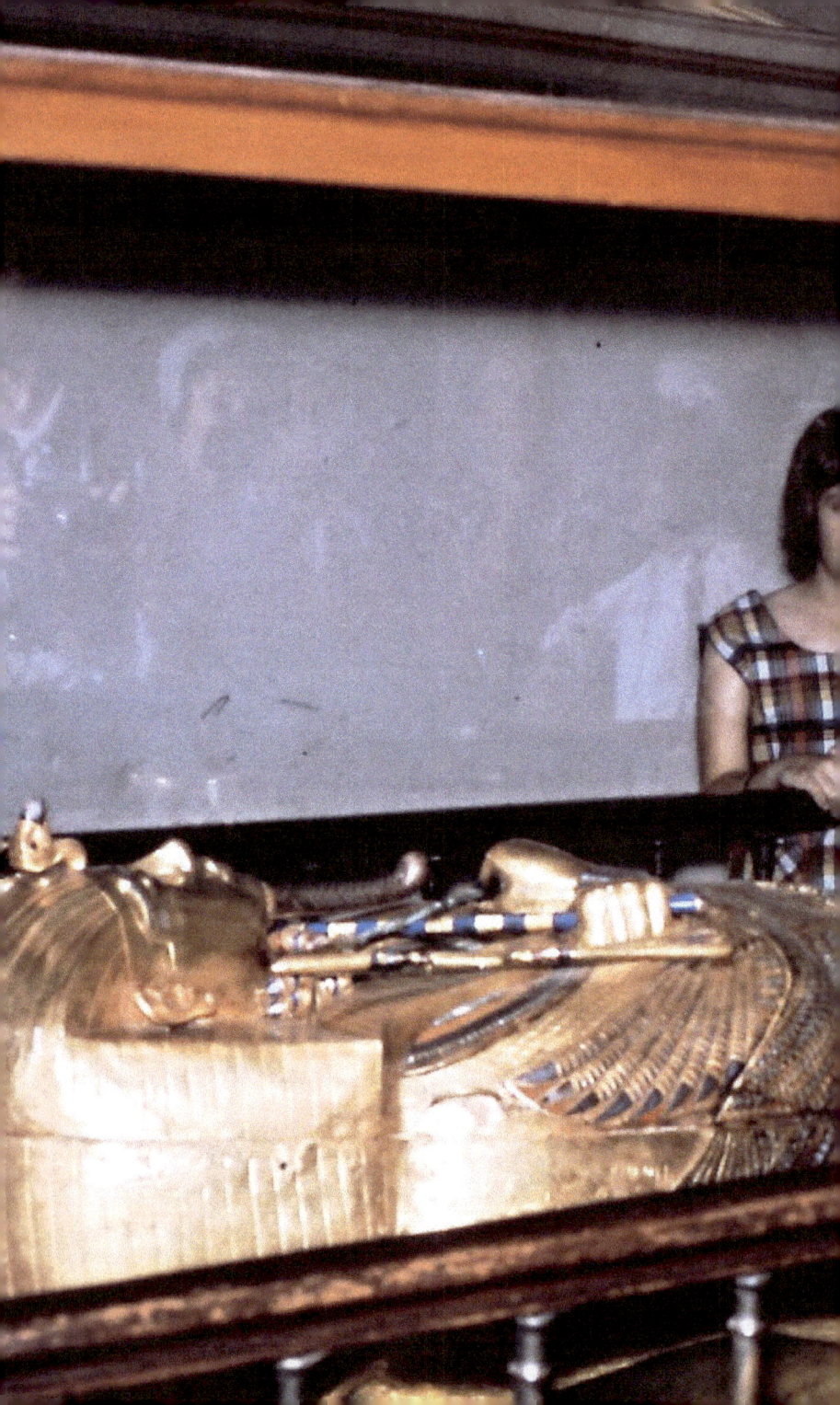

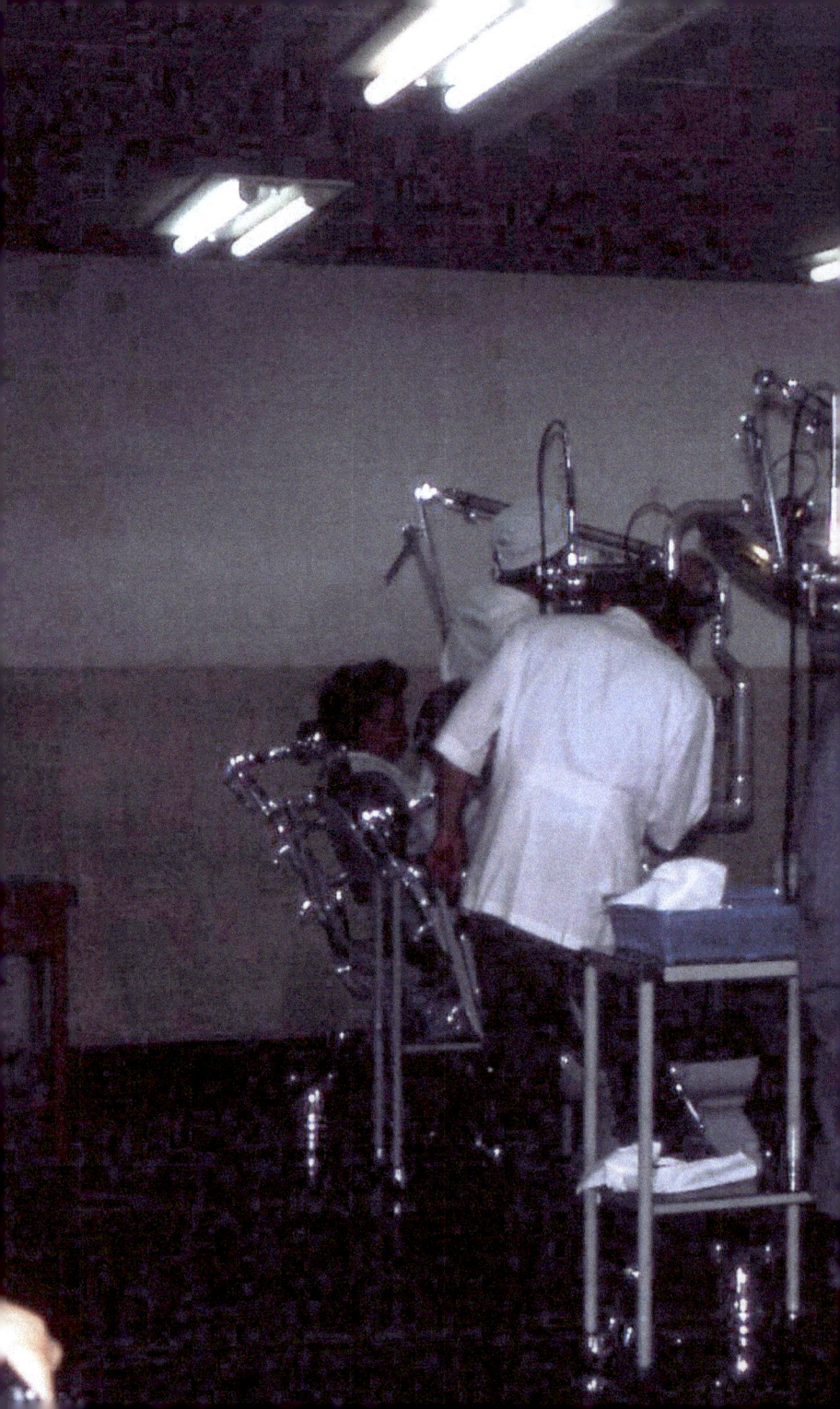

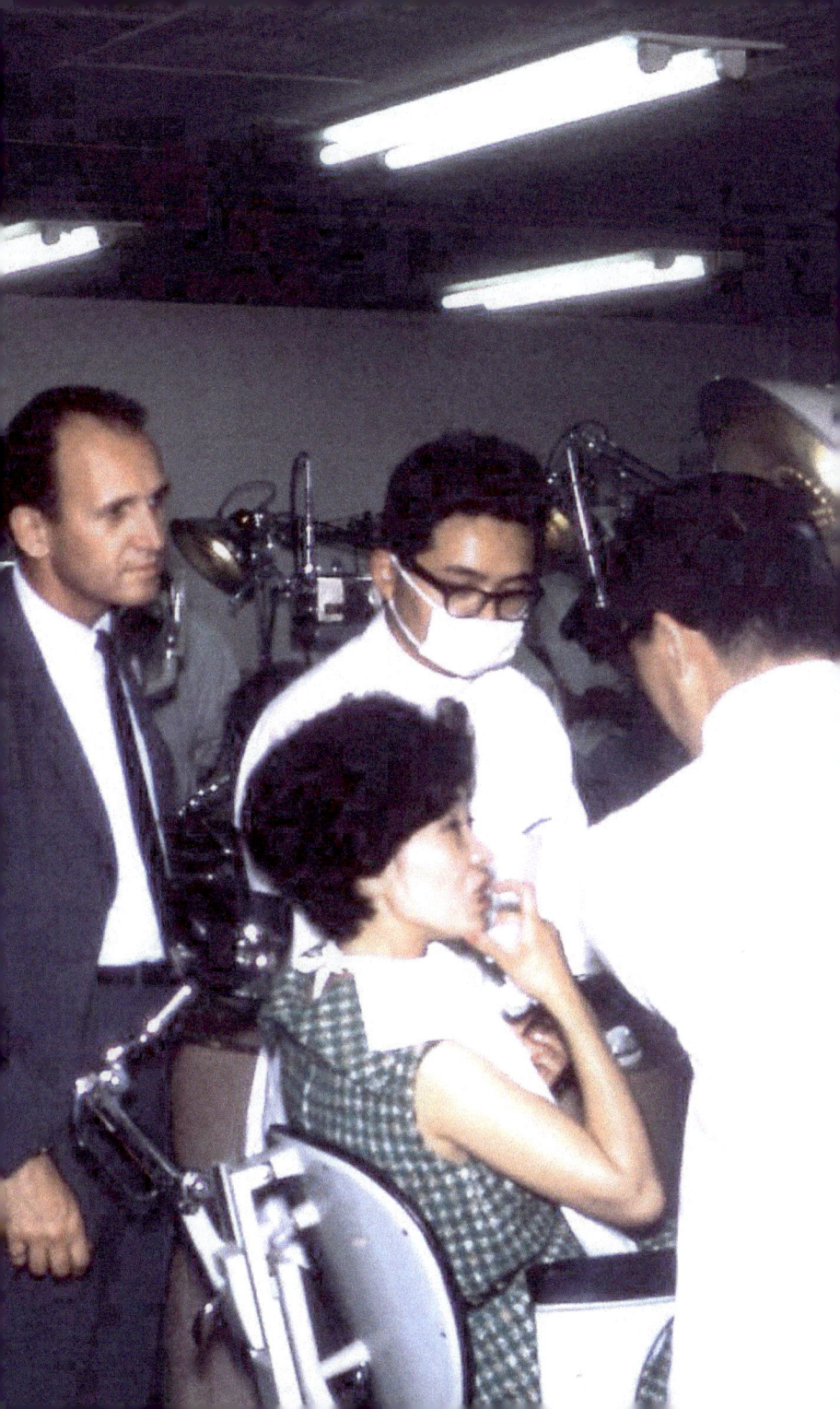

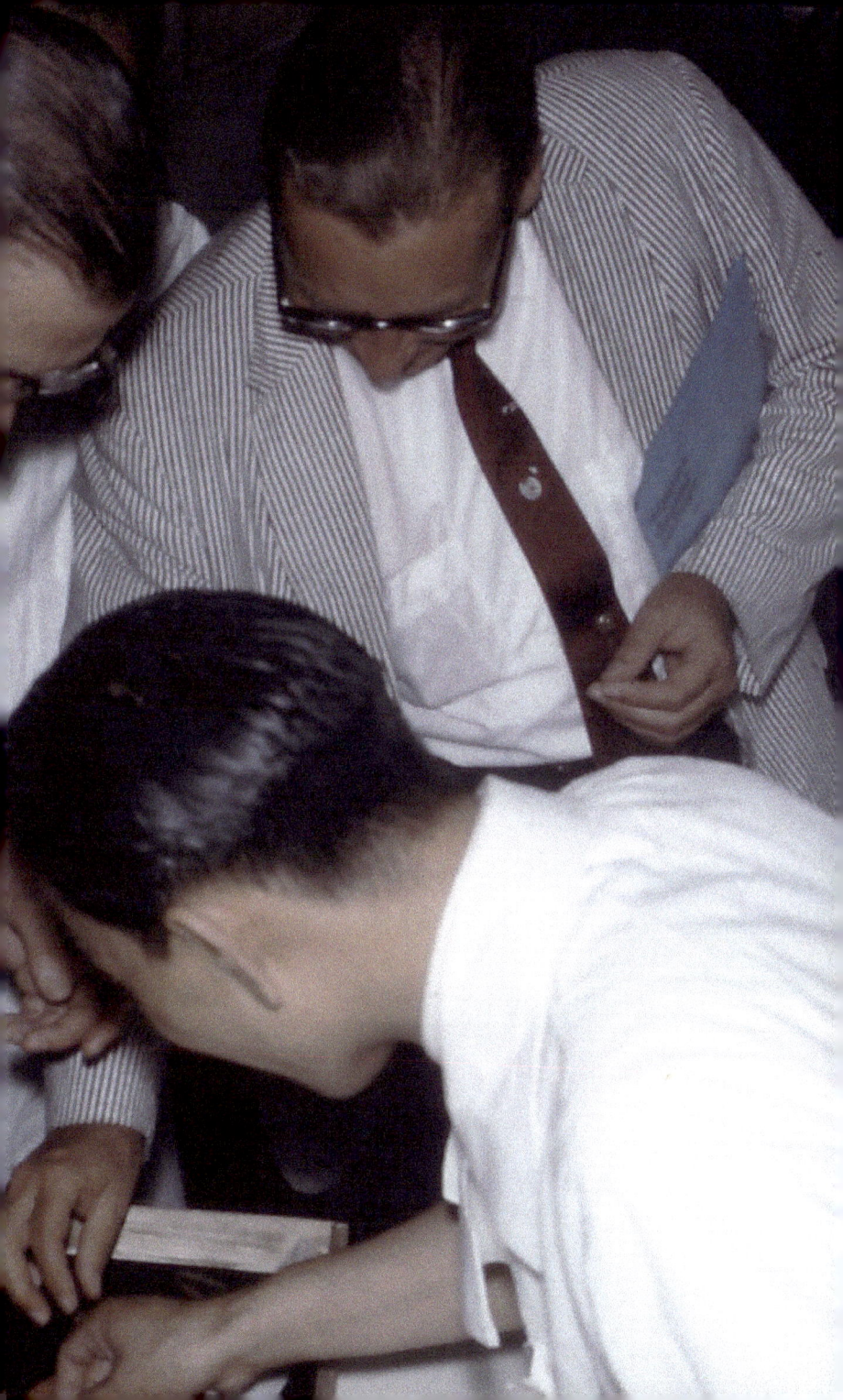

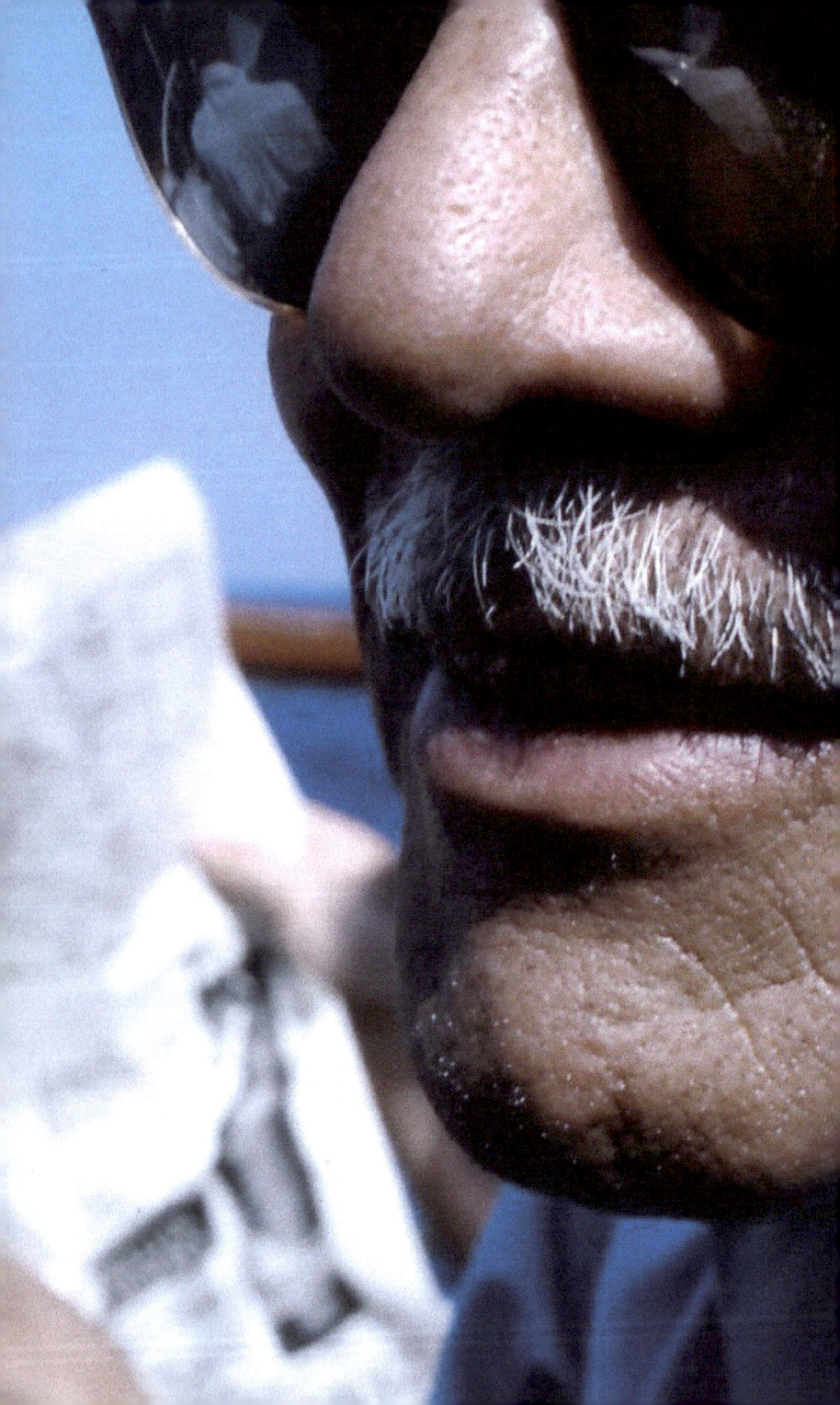

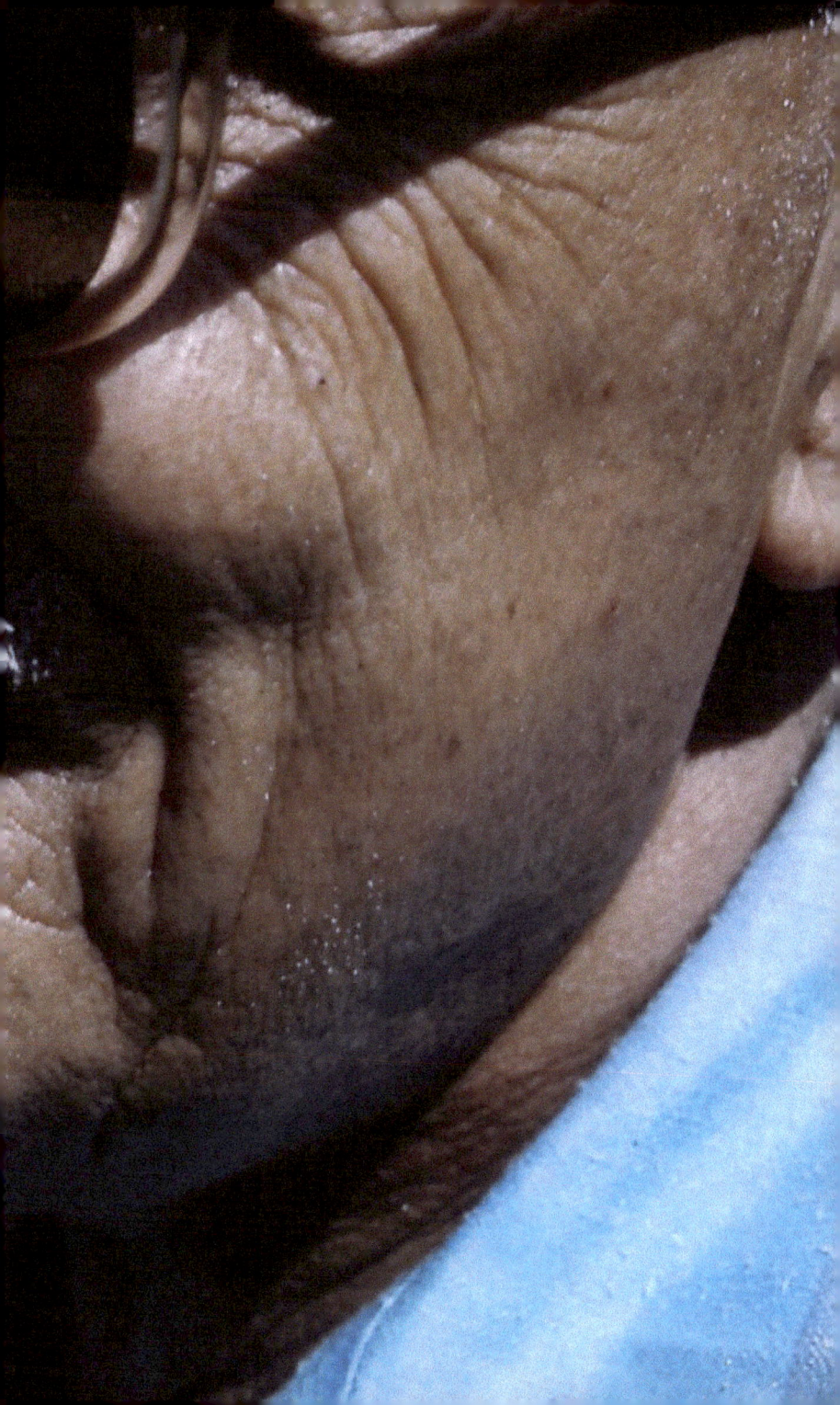

1427
AÇORES

MADEIR

I.ᴬˢ C.º VERDE

PORTUGAL

1434
C. BOJADOR
1441

1444
CABO VERDE

GUINE
1460

147
MINA

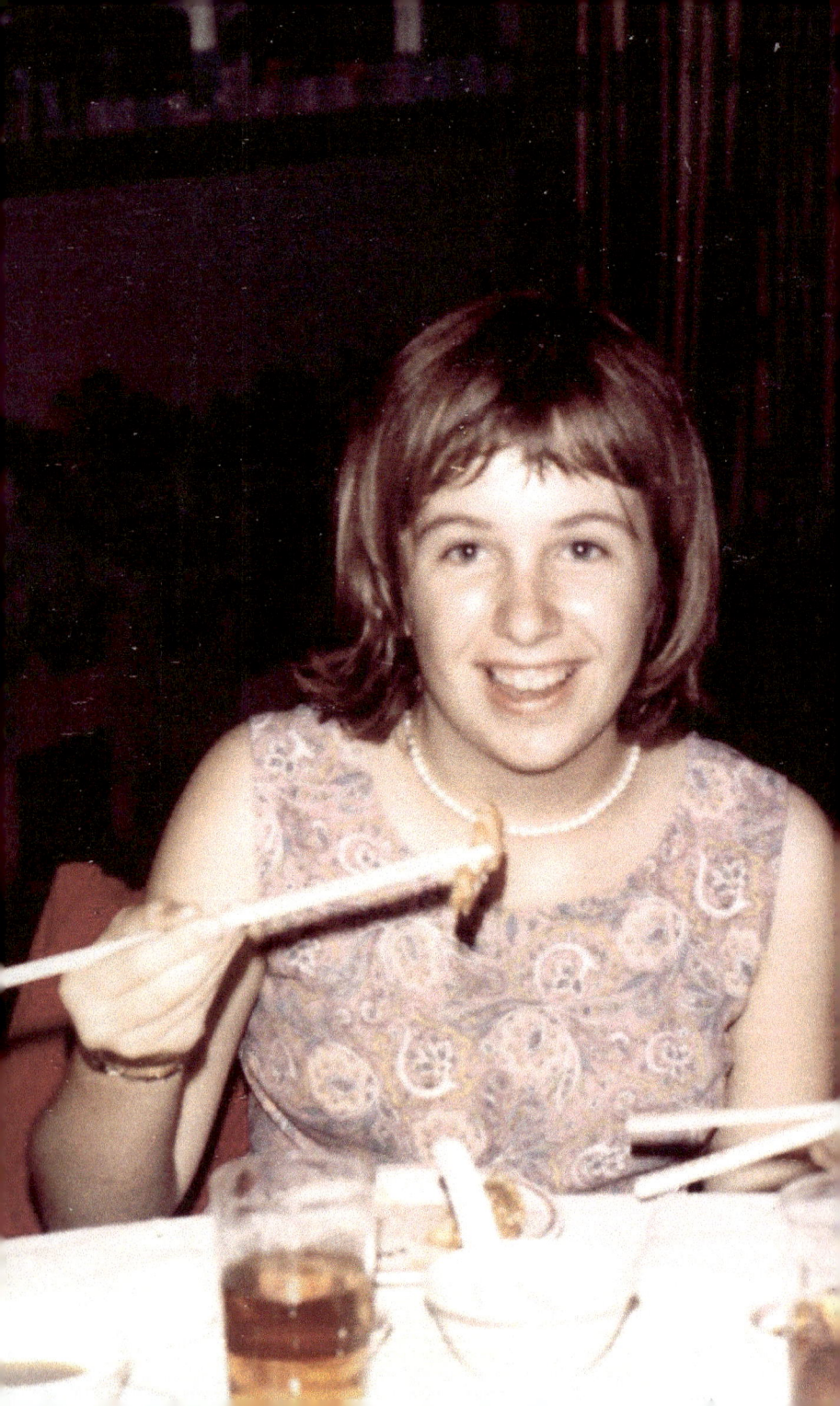

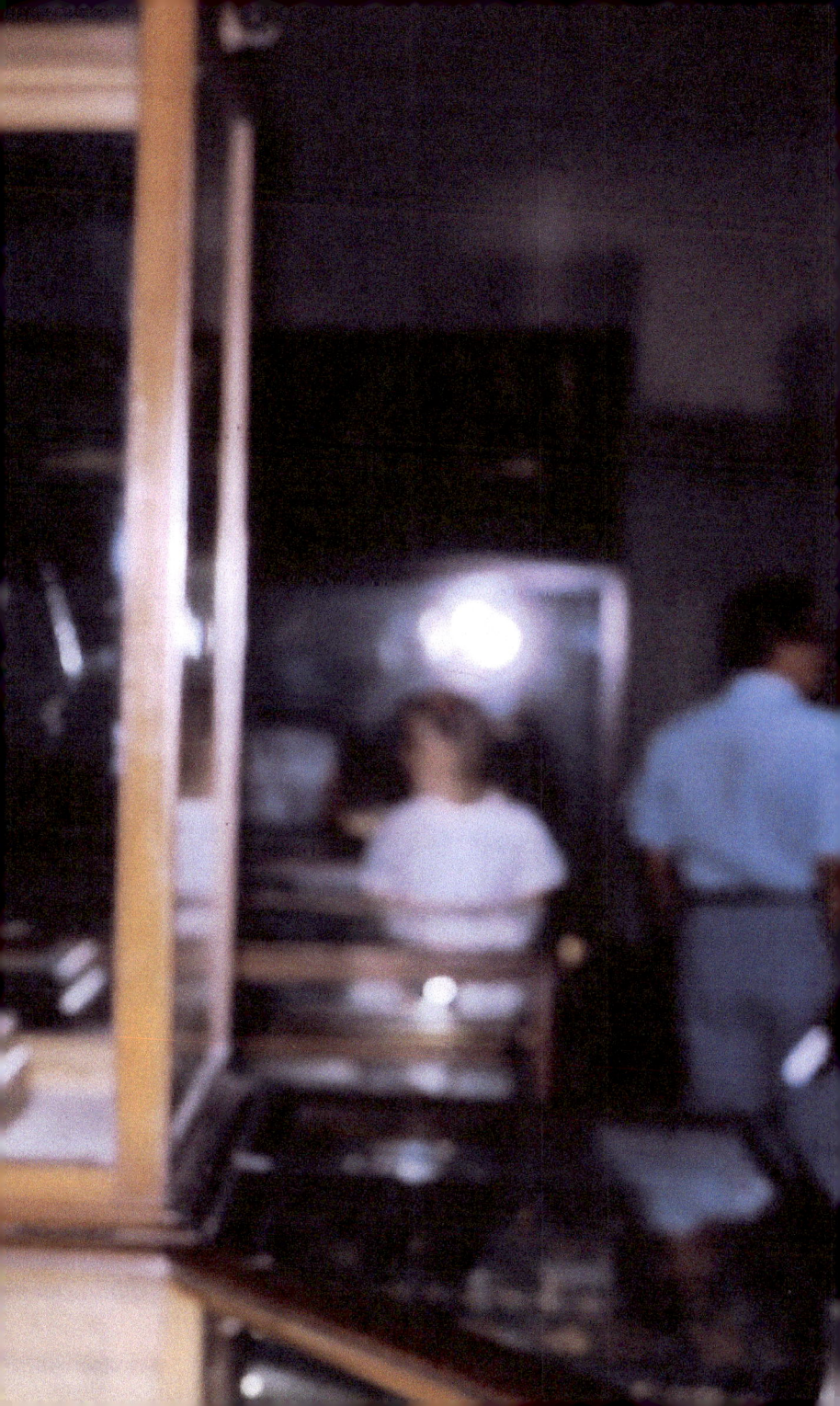

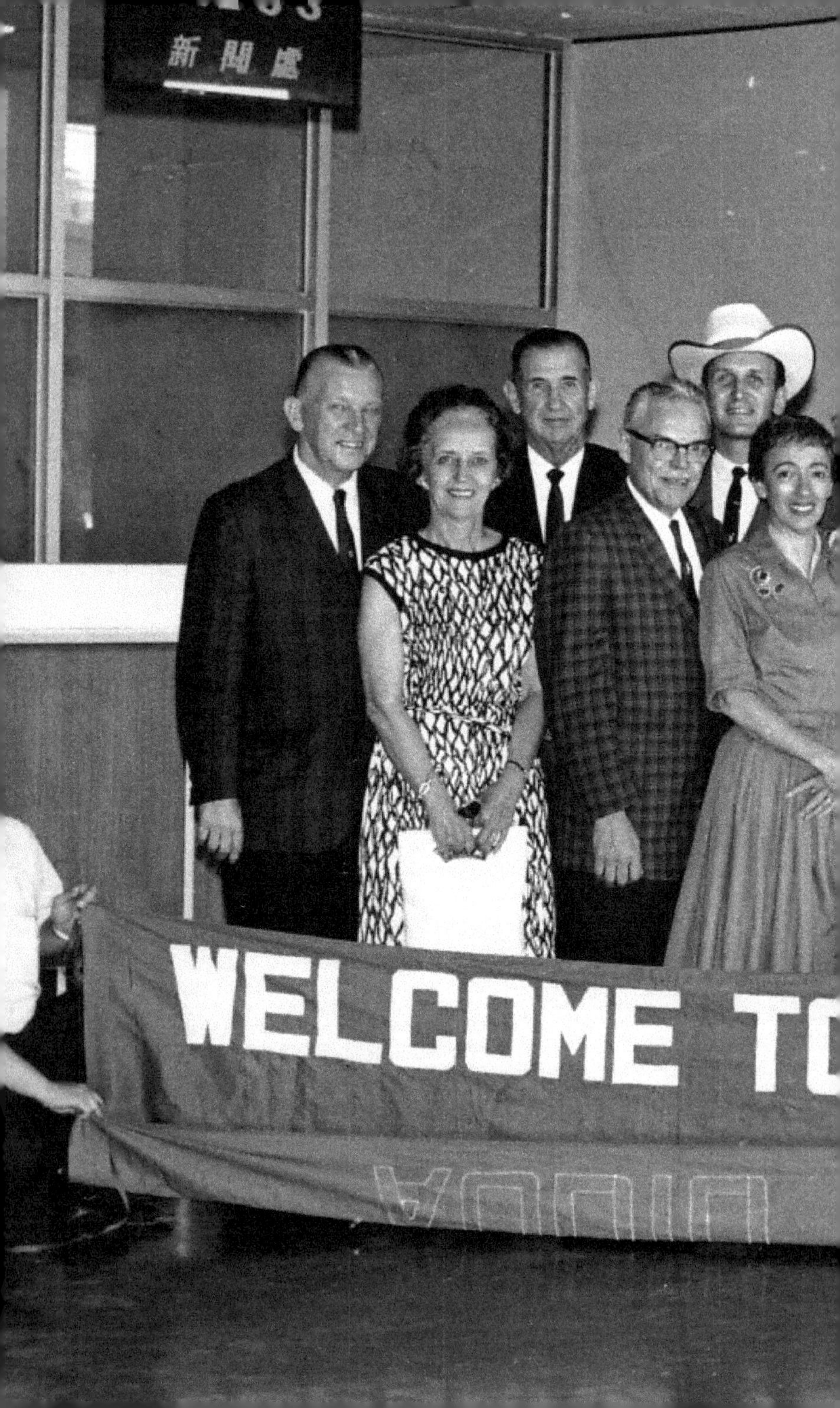
新聞處
WELCOME T

HONG KONG

WONDERFUL
WORLD OF
DENTISTRY TOUR

WONDERFUL
WORLD OF
DENTISTRY TOUR

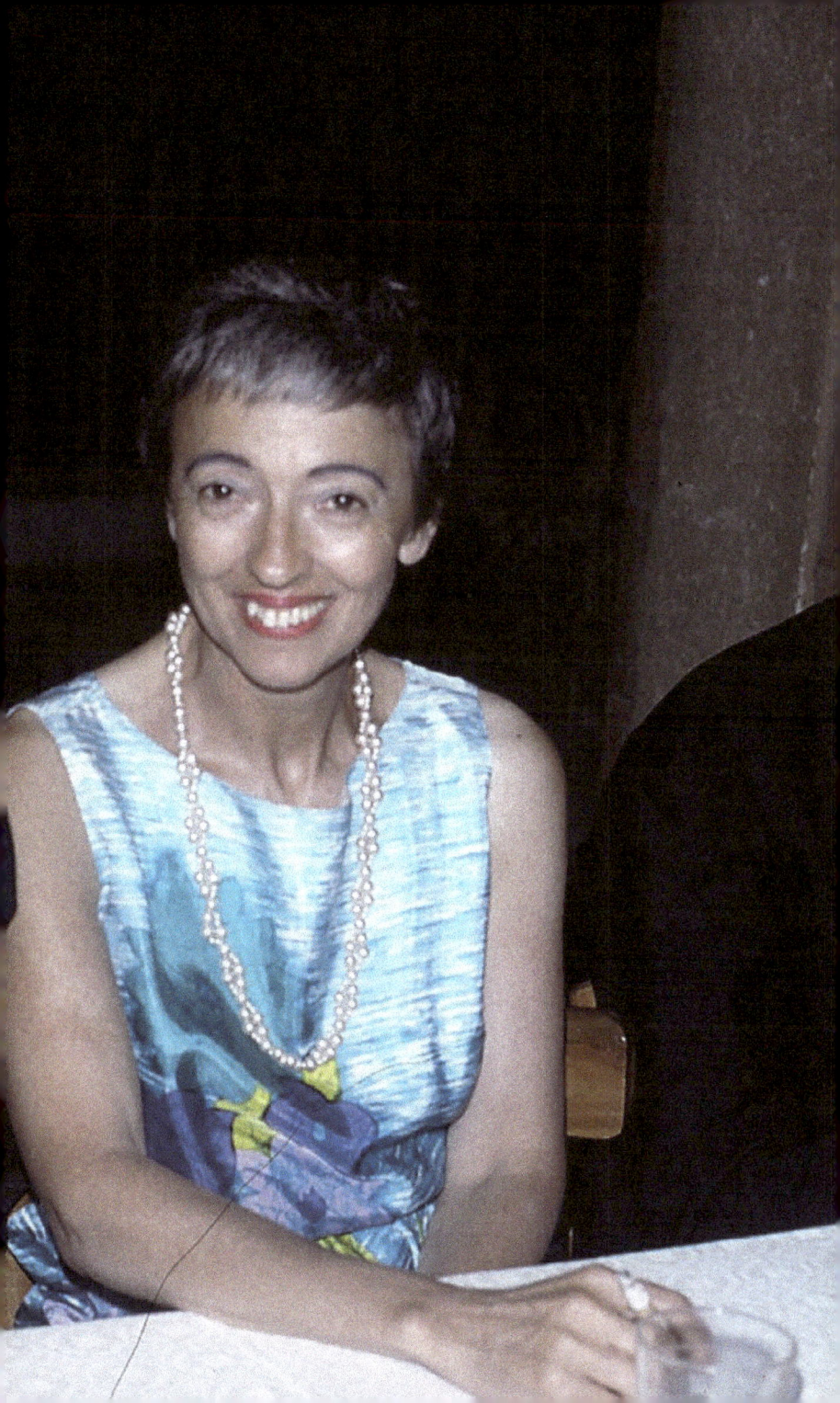

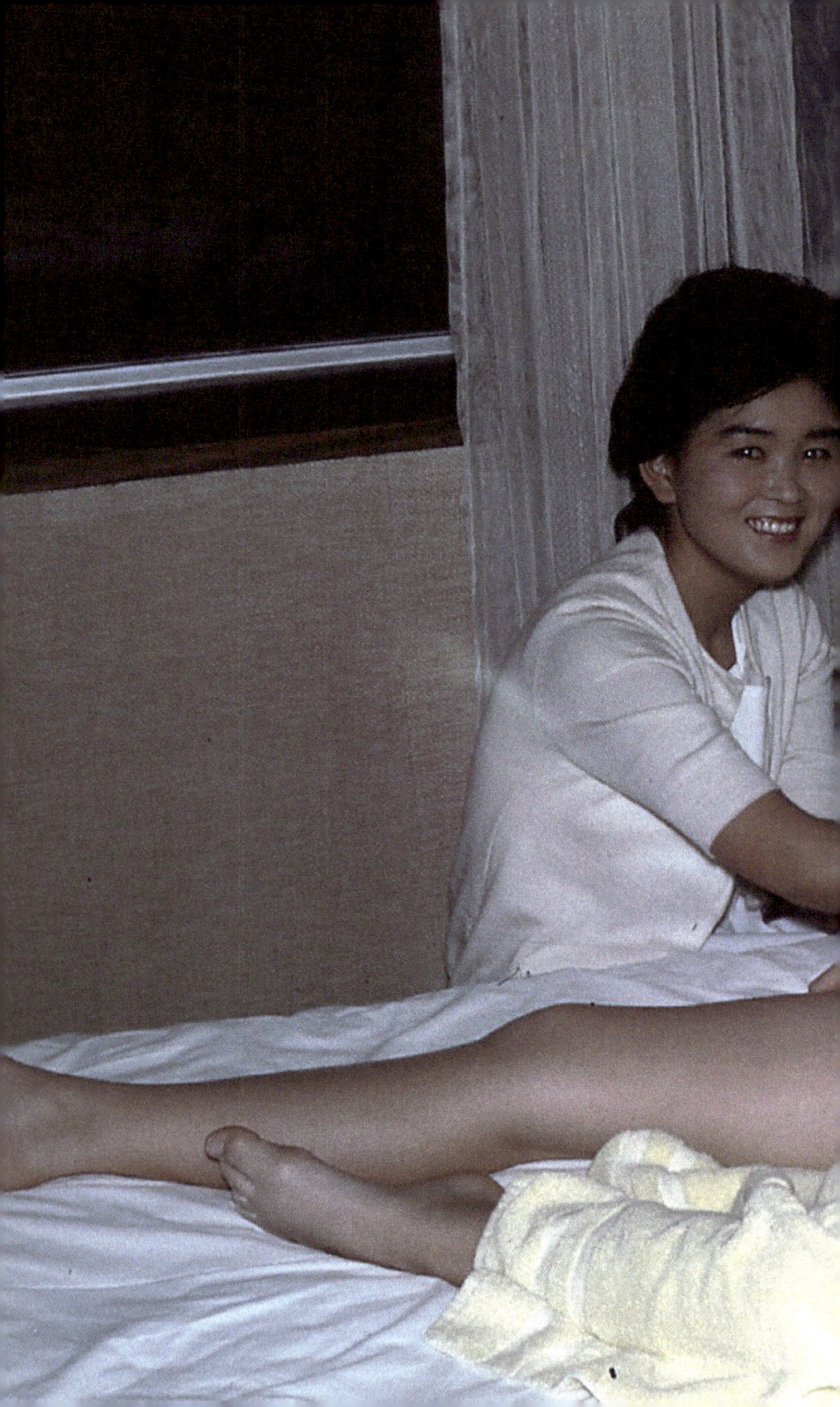

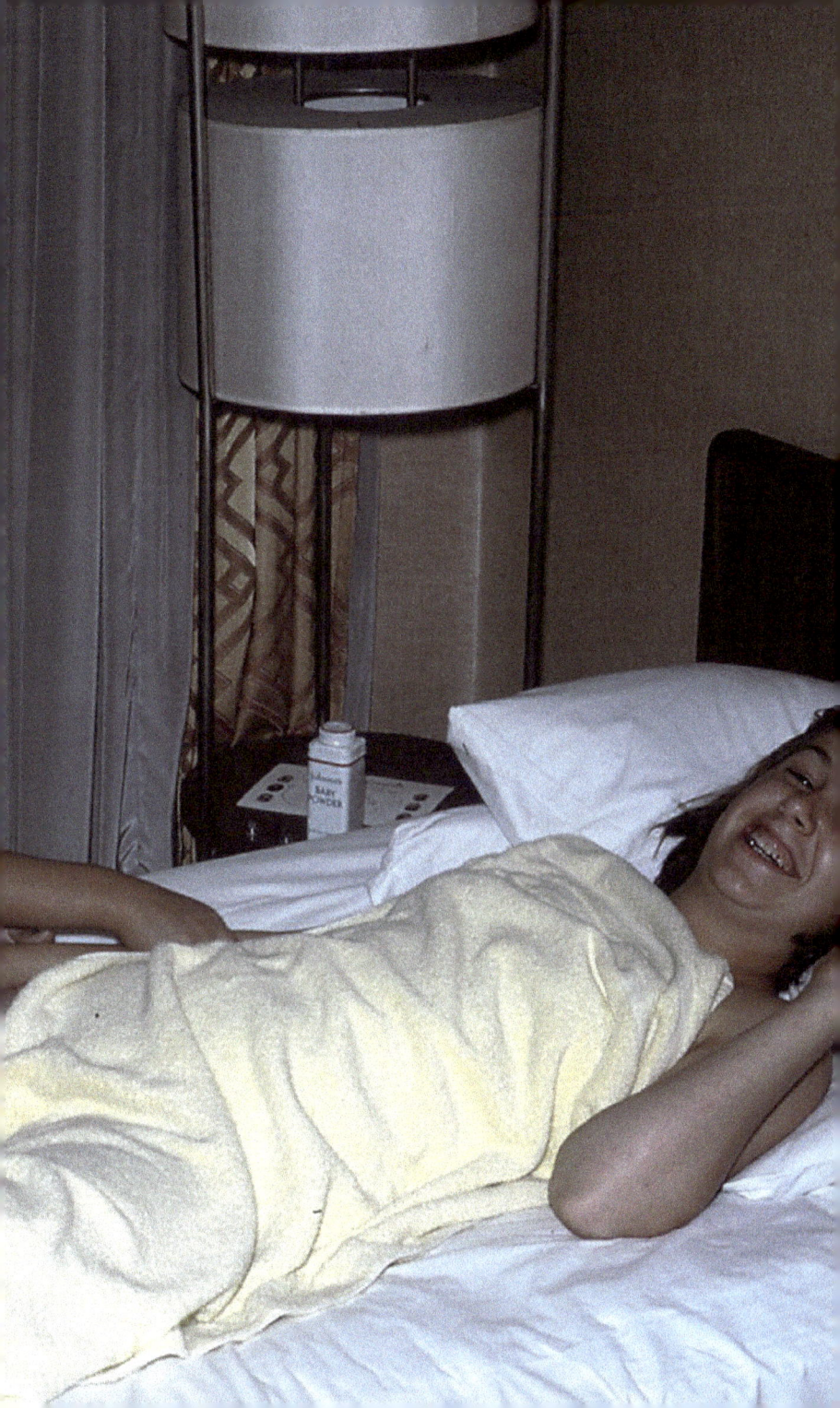

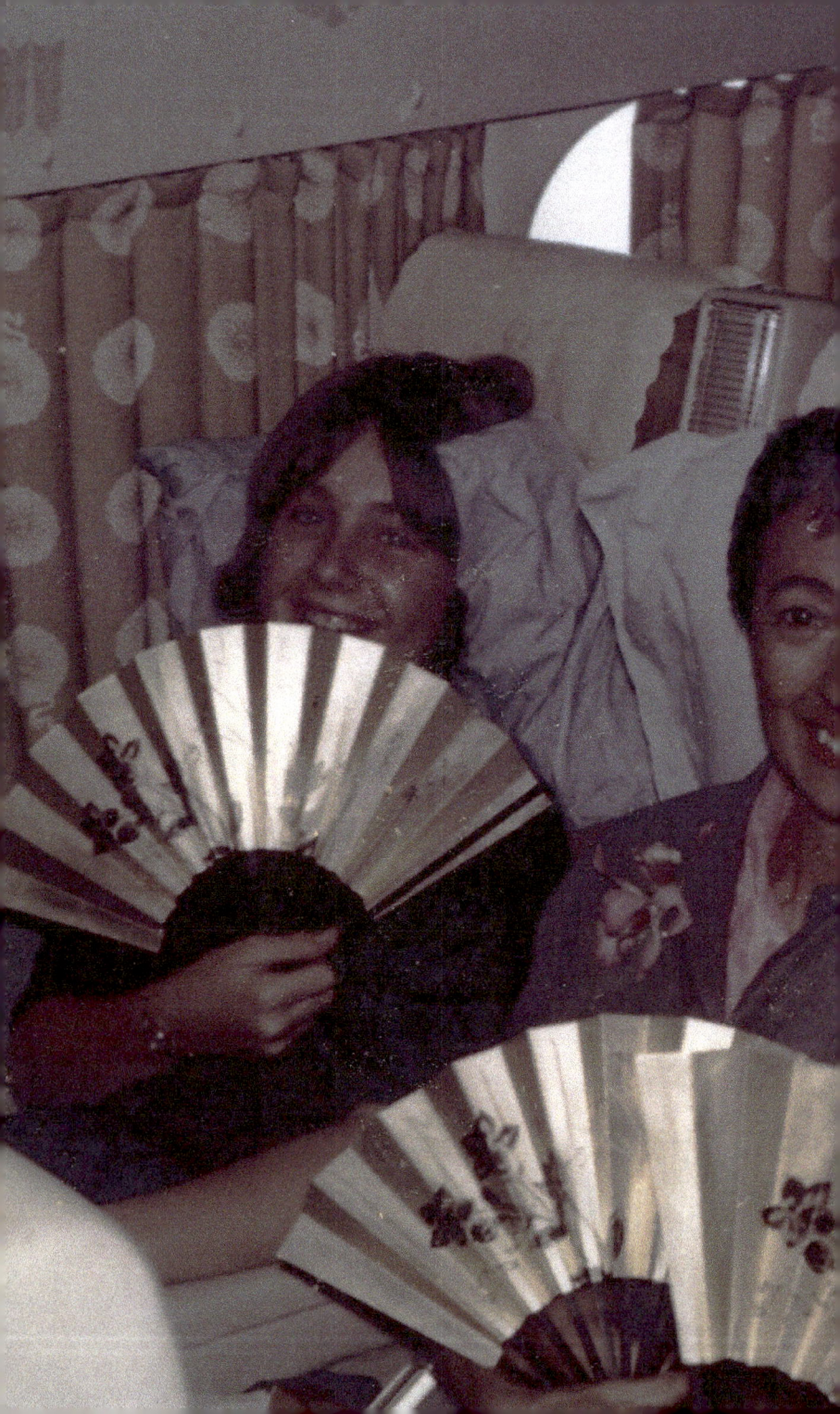

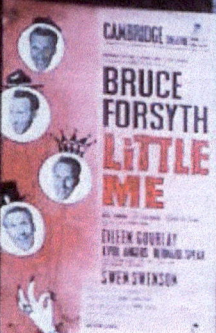

CAMBRIDGE THEATRE

BRUCE FORSYTH

LiTTLE ME

EILEEN GOURLAY
APRIL ANGERS · WISOLD SPEAR
SWEN SWENSON

DAVE KING

A FUNNY THING
HAPPENED ON THE WAY TO THE FORUM

PETER O'TOOLE
WENDY CRAIG
SIAN PHILLIPS
BARBARA JEFFORD
in
Ride a Cock Horse
by DAVID MERCER

New Victoria THEATRE

LONDON'S FESTIVAL BALLET

SWAN LAKE

HAYMARKET THEATRE

MICHAEL DENISON

HOSTILE WITNESS

NOW IN 5 YEAR OF THIS
FIVE STAGE MUSICAL HIT

THE SOUND OF MUSIC

RODGERS & HAMMERSTEIN

LINDSAY & CROUSE

PALACE THEATRE LONDON

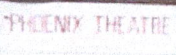

PHOENIX THEATRE

A HERITAGE
and its history

QUEEN'S THEATRE

NIGEL PATRICK   PHYLLIS CALVERT
MAXINE AUDLEY   JOYCE CAREY
RICHARD BRIERS

PRESENT LAUGHTER
NOEL COWARD

Sadler's Wells Theatre

THE BALLET RAMBERT

GLOBE THEATRE

EDITH EVANS
BRIAN AHERNE
and ALAN WEBB
in
THE CHINESE PRIME MINISTER
A NEW PLAY BY ENID BAGNOLD

JOHN OSBORNE

INADMISSIBLE EVIDENCE

COMEDY THEATRE

Spike Milligan
Bill Owen
Valentine Dyall

OBLOMOV

THEATRE TICKETS

REDWOOD SEQUOIA SEMPERVIRENS
WASHED ASHORE AT CRESCENT CITY
DURING THE CHRISTMAS FLOOD OF
1964. PLACED HERE AT THE GATEWAY
TO THE REDWOOD EMPIRE.
• MAY 10 1965 •

SHRI LAKSHMI NARA

BUILT 1936 A.D. 199

THIS TEMPLE IS BUILT FOR SHRI SANATAN DHARAM S
RAJA BALDEV DASS BIRLA. ALL HINDUS OF ALL B
DHARAM INCLUDING ARYA, BAUDH, JAIN SIKH IM
WORSHIP, SATSANG AND KIRTAN IN CONSONANCE W
TEMPLE IN MUTUAL HARMONY AND GOOD WILL.

THIS TEMPLE IS OPEN TO ALL HINDUS INCLUDIN
PRESCRIBED CONDITIONS OF CLEANLINESS, FULL FA
PERSONS SUFFERING FROM INFECTIOUS DISEA
ALLOWED IN OR NEAR THE TEMPLE.

NOTE - NONE BUT THE MANAGEMENT SHALL INTER
WHICH SHALL BE CONDUCTED ACCORDING TO SANAT

...MPLE

...DELHI BY SHRI SETH
...F SHRI SANATAN
...PATE IN THE DAILY
...NVENTIONS OF THE

...IS SUBJECT TO THE
...NCERE DEVOTION
...GGARS ARE NOT

...E WORSHIP OF THE TEMPLE
...RITES AND OBSERVANCES

CPSIA information can be obtained
at www.ICGtesting.com
Printed in the USA
BVHW091433290719
554569BV00011B/427/P